D1109149

ANADIAN
TAIN HOLIDAYS

-HIKING &
TAINEERING

I believe the mountains' stalwart stature reminds us of precious moments and times that seem to be hidden from us in our day to day lives. A day spent in the mountains, experiencing the endless variety of changes taking place with the weather, light, flowers and wildlife, is as close to a full battery recharge as one can get today. — Mark Kingsbury

In memory of Mark Kingsbury
CMH President 1991 - 2001

The whole world became one of mountain-top islands punctuating a sea of clouds. The feeling on top will forever be with me as an indescribable blend of photographic beauty, joy, accomplishment and insight. — Bruce Allen

HELI-HIKING • MOUNTAINEERING

Box 1660, Banff, Alberta, Canada T1L 1J6
Phone (403) 762-7100 • Fax (403) 762-5879
1-800-661-0252

www.cmhhike.com
www.cmhmountaineering.com

Front cover photograph
*The view from Bugaboo Lodge: Bugaboo Glacier
and Marmolata Spire (3033m)*

Back cover photograph
*The modern-day pack horse: a Bell 212 helicopter
at Cariboo Lodge*

(pp 2/3) Unicorn Glacier in the Adamants

*(pp 4/5) Left to right: Pigeon Spire (3124m), Bugaboo Spire
(3185m), and the Howser Spires (3399m) stand above
Anniversary Glacier in the Bugaboos.*

(above) The Selkirk Range in the Adamants

*(opposite) An un-named peak viewed from
Pyrite Ridge in the Adamants*

*Printed in Canada using vegetable-based inks on
Canadian made paper.*

Altitude GreenTree program
*Altitude Publishing will plant twice as many trees
as were used in the manufacturing of this book.*

*Cataloguing in Publication Data
Ettlinger, Catherine
Heli-Hiking and Mountaineering*

ISBN 1-55153-113-5

*1. Mountaineering—British Columbia—Pictorial works.
2. Hiking British Columbia—Pictorial works.
3. CMH Heli-Hiking. I Title. GV199.44.C22B75 2000
796.52'2'09711022   C00-910631-6*

*Design and layout: Stephen Hutchings
Editor: Catherine Ettlinger*

*Altitude Publishing acknowledges the financial support of
the Government of Canada through the Book Publishing
Industry Development Program (BPIDP) for its publishing
activities.*

*Altitude Publishing Canada Ltd.
1500 Railway Ave., Canmore Alberta T1W 1P6
1-800-957-6888 • www.altitudepublishing.com*

HELI-HIKING &
MOUNTAINEERING

Contents

We experienced the mountains in all their varied majesty: cold, hot, sunny, snowy, gray, and colorfully flower-bedecked....CMH stretches our capacities, but never too much or too far, in giving us great mountain adventures. — Ann Dodge

Ann Dodge, Jackson, New Hampshire, remembers the thrill of the first three-lodge, Heli-Hiking trip led by Hans Gmoser. Ann was also on Hans' first-ever commercial Heli-Ski trip.

(above) Black Forest Ridge in the Bugaboos

(opposite) Mt. Sir Sandford (3530m) is the highest peak in the Selkirk Range

(pp 10/11) The North and South Canoe Glaciers in the Cariboos

The Birth of Heli-Hiking, Part I

by Hans Gmoser

This is a story about a good idea that went unrecognized at first, and almost failed to come to fruition. I take full responsibility for being the one who didn't want to have anything to do with this good idea...in the beginning.

In April of 1977 my phone rang. A man introduced himself as Arthur Tauck. I had no idea who he was. He told me that he had just spent a week Heli-Skiing with his son in the Cariboos, that they'd had a great experience, and had enjoyed the lodge and the wonderful staff. I politely thanked him for the compliments and said I hoped he'd come again. I was about to hang up when he interrupted and said we might be able to cooperate in a summer business venture.

CMH had tried for several years to generate summer business. We offered horseback riding as well as canoeing and hiking around the Bugaboo and Cariboo Lodges and in the Bugaboos, we even built tennis courts. The net result was that we lost money every summer. By 1977 we had decided to shut everything down in the summer and preserve what money we made in the winter. I wasn't interested in any proposition that would cost us more.

Arthur explained that he operated bus tours in the Canadian Rockies and that he would like to have one of his tours stop at the Cariboo Lodge for a few days. My interest waned even more. I couldn't imagine what we could do with bus-riding, sight-seeing tourists in our mountains. I told him I'd think about it and call him back. We hung up and I promptly forgot the whole thing.

Two weeks later, Arthur called back. He wanted to know what I had been thinking. I crab-danced a little about being too busy, but promised that I would get back to him in a few days. At this point I knew I couldn't get rid of him. I had to start thinking.

Arthur said his tour guests flew to Calgary, and spent two nights each at the Banff Springs Hotel, Chateau Lake Louise and Jasper Park Lodge. He wanted to add two days at the Cariboo Lodge. What could we do with his guests for two days? After some thought, I decided we could fly them directly from the Jasper Park Lodge to the Cariboo Lodge. With 40 people going each way, at 10 per flight, that would take care of one day. The next day we could have nature talks in the lodge, and then fly everyone around in the helicopter to look at the mountains.

After all this profound thinking I called Arthur. "No, no!" he said. "Why don't you do the same thing you do in winter? Fly the people up to some beautiful place, let them go for a walk, and then move on to another place." Well, this short explanation turned the light on for me.

Arthur would come to Banff. I would gather a few people representative of his clientele, we'd fly to the Cariboos, and see how they reacted. Arthur also asked me to invite Ivor Petrak, the Vice President and General Manager of the Canadian Pacific Mountain Hotels, because in order for this tour to work, he needed a commitment for more rooms in these hotels. At the moment he was already at the limit of what they would give him.

It was a beautiful July day in 1977 when we flew from Banff to the Cariboos. After a quick lunch at the lodge we visited three different landing sites. Everyone was ecstatic about their experience.

Among our guests was Lizzie Rummel who had spent most of her life skiing, hiking and climbing. Now, with one fused hip, severe arthritis and approaching 80, she returned to places she never expected to visit again.

Back in Banff, Arthur, Ivor and I sat down to see how we could make this work. Ivor was brief. He simply said, "Arthur, you've got your rooms." With that hurdle out of the way, Arthur and I agreed that he would do the packaging, marketing and selling of this tour, while CMH would provide the ground service for guests at the lodge. This included helicopter transport to and from the highway, two nights at the lodge, all meals (wine with dinner), and guided hikes from six different helicopter landing sites.

The first summer, 1978, the Cariboo Lodge operated at 87% occupancy. The following year, Arthur achieved 100% occupancy, and we were talking about expanding this operation to the Bugaboo Lodge. By the summer of 1982, Heli-Hiking was offered at the Cariboo, Bugaboo and Bobbie Burns Lodges.

In promoting Heli-Hiking, Arthur was very careful in explaining the experience and what people needed to bring. He supplied a small packsack, a warm parka and rain gear. In the brochure he stated that guests needed to bring good, sturdy walking shoes. Understanding the meaning of good, sturdy walking shoes varied widely among our guests. The first summer I literally carried one lady down a steep, grassy slope in her gem-studded, black satin loafers.

When I asked if she'd read about bringing good, sturdy walking shoes, she said "These are my walking shoes."

Arthur, always wanting to do the best for his guests, bought a whole inventory of light mountain hiking boots, which were kept at the lodge.

We were dealing with people who'd never seen mountains except from a distance. Yet we had them walking through alpine meadows covered with beautiful flowers, hiking along high ridges, crossing snowfields, all in the heart of exceedingly beautiful and spectacular mountain scenery. This was an experience far beyond anything they had ever imagined. As a group, their enthusiasm and their sense of accomplishment was far greater than that of our skiers. For us, it was highly rewarding to give such intense pleasure to so many.

I felt that this activity could be enjoyed by far more people than Heli-Skiing. We could accommodate virtually any physical limitation. And, we could also make this very exciting and demanding for the most accomplished mountaineers. In other words, we could provide a great adventure for the whole spectrum of people who enjoy being in the mountains in the summer.

The challenge was how to position this experience in the marketplace. Immediately we found that we had literally fallen between the chairs. The perception about Heli-Hiking ranged from "This is way too tough" to "This is a real Mickey Mouse activity." While Arthur was very success-

ful in filling our three lodges with Heli-Hikers, his success was largely based on the tremendous loyalty he'd built up among his clientele. Many came because this was a new Tauck Tour—they'd already been on 20 others—and if it was a Tauck Tour it must be good.

We had almost no success in attracting others in the beginning. Very, very slowly word got out that, "Hey, this is a great way to do something active and challenging in beautiful, remote mountain country...and have a very comfortable, well-run lodge to live in." All of a sudden word of mouth kicked in. Demand grew steadily and now CMH offers a whole palette of summer mountain activities.

Had it not been for Arthur Tauck, his vision, his perseverence, his unfailing desire to always do the right thing for his guests, and his highly ethical way of doing business, instead of Heli-Hiking we may have had just another variety of Flight-Seeing. Thank you Arthur!

(above) Margaret and Hans Gmoser in the Cariboos

The Author
Hans Gmoser is the founder of CMH Heli-Skiing and Heli-Hiking.

The Birth of Heli-Hiking, Part II

by Arthur Tauck

For anyone to effectively understand my involvement with CMH and the subsequent birth of Heli-Hiking as I envisioned it, one must first realize that I operate tours in the Canadian Rockies as well as many other destinations around the world.

I am also a skier. In 1975 my wife and I spent a month hopscotching our way north from Salt Lake City to Jasper, sampling various ski resorts along the way. By the time we reached Jasper we were about skied out. While my wife elected to take a couple of days off, I set out to explore the possibility of Heli-Skiing.

I had heard about Heli-Skiing in the Bugaboos, but knew nothing about CMH. Believe it or not I turned to the Banff Yellow Pages and that's how I found out about CMH. When I asked about Heli-Skiing for a day, they suggested I head for Valemount early the next morning to join a group of doctors who were skiing the Cariboos from the Sarac Motel.

With my 220cm Hexel Competition skis and nervous as hell, I joined that group. It wasn't long before I realized I had the wrong equipment. Regardless, I found myself experiencing something extraordinary, something that challenged all of my senses far beyond anything I'd ever done before.

At lunch we joined the group from the Cariboo Lodge, and I couldn't help but appreciate the bonding, spirit and camaraderie among the lodge guests. There was something very special going on. You could sense it in the air.

Late that afternoon on the drive back to Jasper, I vowed to return the following year with my son Chuck, who would then be due a college graduation present.

It was April 1976 when we joined Kiwi Gallagher and his staff for a Heli-Ski week in the Cariboos—it proved far more exhilarating than I had ever expected. I was amazed at the construction of the lodge, the comfort of the accommodations, and the sophistication of the cuisine. Plus, that something special I felt the year before was still in the air, and the skiing was only part of it. The social chemistry among the group was intense.

Tour operators strive to enhance the social chemistry among their guests. Sometimes we are more successful than other times, but even at our best, nothing matched what I experienced in the Cariboos that week. My son and I became one with the other guests. We lived the experience of a lifetime together. It became clear to me that CMH had found the solution to packaging magic.

I simply could not get the feeling out of my head. I asked whether the lodges were open in summer and learned they were not. This started my juices churning.

Could I combine the CMH experience with a motorcoach tour of the Rockies and thus free up some of the coveted hotel inventory that could then be utilized to add more departures to our other Rocky programs?

Much of any tour operator's success in the Rockies is limited by the number of hotel rooms he controls in Banff and Jasper National Parks, or specifically for my company, Tauck Tours, at the Banff Springs Hotel, Chateau Lake Louise and Jasper Park Lodge. Due to building limitations imposed by Parks Canada, there has always been more demand for rooms than there has been supply. This is especially true during the peak summer months.

There was another question in my mind, too: would the senior citizens we cater to appreciate a mountain program given the frailties of age?

Coincidentally, about this time, I happened to visit my wife's 97-year-old grandmother, who was in a home living out her waning days. It was a sad visit. She was failing fast. Among her last words to me were, "Arthur, inside this baggy old body of bones, I am still 25." I cried, and later realized she had answered one of my questions.

We had always designed tours around our perception of our elderly clientele's physical limitations. Maybe that was a mistake. My grandmother-in-law convinced me that we should let our clients determine their own limitations. We should design tours that would engage their spirit and tenacity, that would leave them with a renewed pride in themselves.

I tracked down this guy Hans Gmoser. I wanted to talk to him about my idea of introducing my clients to his lodges and letting them partake of the magic and purity of an alpine experience geared to their wishes and capabilities. I envisioned a program like Hans' Heli-Skiing where each day guests are divided by ability and heli-lifted to four or five different venues they could explore with a guide.

Suffice it to say that Hans was not easy to convince, but that's another story for another day. Ultimately, we met and flew to the Cariboos to better understand each other and explore the possibility of working together. Hans, the skeptic, soon became Hans, the enthusiast.

Next, we both realized that our enthusiasm for Heli-Hiking had to pass the test of reality. We looked at each other and, both understanding the business risk involved, decided to go forward.

The next summer, 1978, with a single mailing to Tauck customers, we introduced 900 people to the mountain magic of the Cariboos. The following summer we maximized the capacity of the Cariboo Lodge with over 1200 guests. This encouraged expansion to the Bugaboos, and later the Bobbie Burns. Both Hans and I fed on the positive feedback we received from our guests.

In reality we were challenging the majority of our guests to participate in situations that were but a few inches over their heads, even though they felt they were into something miles above them. If

they were stymied physically, we didn't rush to their aid. We let them figure it out, but always under the guide's watchful eye. Aid came when needed, but in most cases our guests accomplished the tasks themselves.

The result was a renewed sense of pride. They met the challenge of satisfying their inner spirit at a time in their lives when they were beginning to accept the more sedentary life that comes with age. It was a joy to watch them fanny-slide down snowy slopes, frolic like kids with snowballs in the midst of summer, and push themselves along the ridgelines and up the slopes far above timber. They learned about the flora, fauna and the power of glaciation. They embraced the mountain environment...and they bonded with one another and wished they could adopt the CMH staff that made it all possible.

Then, upon departure, while waiting for the helicopter

to return them to reality, I would witness reflection, sometimes tearful. Maybe it was about their accomplishments and the fact that they may never have such an experience again.

I too, have found myself with moist eyes: seeing their emotion, I realized that Hans and I were the architects of an experience that enhanced and sometimes changed the lives of many.

We have watched, awestruck, amputees navigate the meadows and the glaciers. We have seen the more fit eagerly reach out to embrace the challenges of mountaineering. And we have witnessed families unite with teenagers, parents and grandparents, each at their own level of participation, but each sharing the same emotion.

My original goal of creating Heli-Hiking to take advantage of added rooms in the Rockies for financial gain has long since faded in importance. As it has turned out, my personal gain is the realization that Heli-Hiking has rekindled the dreams that reside in so many of us. My only regret is that my wife's 97-year-old grandmother never had the chance to live the experience she inspired. God bless her.

(above) Arthur Tauck in the Bugaboos

The Author
Arthur Tauck is the second of three generations to own and manage Tauck Tours, the world's first motor coach tour company.

(top) Alpine fireweed and arnica flourish beside an alpine brook

(bottom) Alpine meadow in the Adamants

(opposite) On the North Canoe Glacier in the Cariboos

(above) Triangular leaf rag-wort and alpine fireweed

(bottom) Alpine fireweed and Indian paintbrush

(opposite) Many lasting friendships are made

(pg 20) A young mule deer surrounded by false hellebore

(pg 21) Bear tracks in the snow

No trail mars the untrammeled quality of the scene. The only signs of previous visitation are a two-foot-deep hole scoured by a brown bear and occasional mountain goat droppings.— Christina Williams

Christina Williams is a freelance writer from Aurora, Colorado

(top) A ptarmigan in her summer plummage

(bottom) A young black bear looks for berries.

(opposite) Nanny and kid mountain goats

(top) A young moose

(bottom) Hoary marmot
(Whistle pig)

(opposite) Bald eagle

Jaws dropped as we banked over alpine firs, crested razor-sharp ridges and swirled above rumpled white glaciers. Our IMAX-view flight ended in a 'Sound of Music' meadow called International Basin. Again, we heli-huddled until our pilot disappeared over the peaks. — Barb and Ron Kroll

Barb and Ron Kroll are freelance writers and photographers from Toronto, Ontario

(top) Heli-huddle in the Adamants

(bottom) Playing in glacial silt

(opposite) Eric Unterberger, manager of the Adamant Lodge, and his group smile for the camera.

27

A Perfect
Heli-Hiking Day

The helicopter lifts off leaving you and your group alone in a vast alpine wilderness. Across the valley is a 1,000 year old glacier; next to you is a sheer rock face that begs to be climbed. With the assistance of the experienced guide, you reach a nearby ridge and look down at a stream twisting through the valley a mile below you. You ford a river, stop for lunch and then explore an alpine meadow for exquisite wildflowers. At the end of the day, the helicopter returns to whisk you back to the comfort of your lodge, the pleasure of a gourmet dinner and the warmth of sharing your experiences with friends.

Flying from Valemount Lodge deep into the Cariboo Mountains

The first landing!

A morning hike in the high meadows

Hands-on lunch-time fun

Rappelling to dessert

Spectacular views at lunch

Exploring a new alpine environment after lunch

The helicopter on its way to pick up another group

Return to the helicopter for a ride back to the lodge

A toast to a perfect day in the mountains

The Lodges of CMH

*(above) Cariboo Lodge look-
ing up the Canoe Valley*

(top right) Bugaboo Lodge

*(bottom) Looking towards
"Vertigo" from the deck of
the Bobbie Burns Lodge*

*(top) Valemount Lodge
dining room*

*(middle) Bugaboo Glacier
from the Bugaboo Lodge
living room*

*(bottom) Cariboo Lodge
bedroom*

(top left) Whirlpool at
Bobbie Burns Lodge

(top right) Climbing wall at
the Adamant Lodge

(bottom) CMH chefs' annual
meeting

*Our only complaint...all that hiking
and we lost not one pound!!!
Too much great food!*
— Dick and Carol Caldwell

The Caldwells live in Westport, Connecticut

*(this page) The healthy gourmet cuisine of the
CMH lodges*

Rolf Regli, mountain guide, plays the Alphorn in the Adamants.

CMH chef Noel Dias prepares a gourmet dinner.

Housekeeper Sarah Blancher prepares for the evening meal.

CMH guides meeting at the Bugaboo Lodge.

Housekeepers Paula Brown and Tanya Schatzmann
prepare your room.

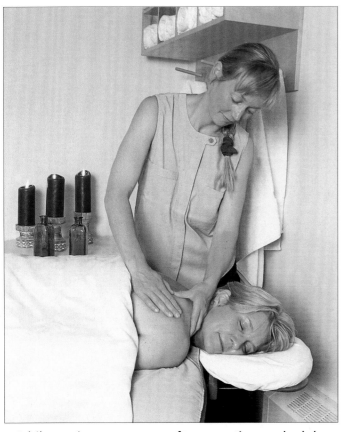

A hiker enjoys a massage after an action-packed day.

CMH maintenance staff Dale Ristau builds a fire.

*Thank you one and all
for the superb care, impeccable
warmth and welcome. It was an
awesome opportunity to see a
part of the world that I could
never have experienced
without you.* — Deborah Davis

Deborah Davis lives in Seattle, Washington

The challenge, the accomplishment, the inner peace, and the higher awareness obtained by climbing these mountains in summer is something no one should miss in a lifetime. — Bruce Allen

(top) Traversing along the lower ridge of Mt. Sir Sandford in the Adamants

(bottom) A view from the summit of Remillard Peak towards Hitchhiker Peak in the Adamants

(top) Top-roping at a small rock bluff in Stitt Creek, Adamants

(bottom) Beginner rock climbing in the Cariboos

(pg 38) Crevasse on the North Canoe Glacier, Cariboos

(pg 39) A glacial millwell

A Heli-Skier Becomes a Heli-Hiker

by Catherine Ettlinger

Was I ever wrong about Heli-Hiking. I had always thought of it more for first-time mountaineers (read "motor-coach tourists") than for serious adventurers (read "Heli-Skiers"). No more. There were days Heli-Hiking in the Bugaboos and the Bobbie Burns that made the 14,000 vertical feet I skied my first day out one year in the Cariboos seem like child's play...or the week I skied 200,000 vertical feet in the Bobbie Burns seem a no greater challenge than the bunny slope. Really.

Thanks to summer light, Heli-Hiking days are long and more often than not, my group came in as the stars were coming out. As with Heli-Skiing, lodge guests are divided into groups according to ability and how much energy they want to expend. While many of the hikers were merely meandering, and were simply out to enjoy a once-in-a-lifetime view, my group was serious. The hiking was arduous and required every bit of stamina (and returned every bit of excitement) as skiing the trees. But there's no time to catch your breath while someone else is hunting for his skis, or while you're waiting for the helicopter since there is no waiting for the helicopter. This is intense.

We cut our way through dense forests; up craggy escarpments where the pink moss campion, red roseroot, purple sawwort and scorpionweed bloomed among the rocks; and across alpine meadows, lush and green and liberally sprinkled with western anemone, spring beauty, columbine, buttercup, Indian paintbrush and yellow glacier lily. We hiked up peaks where we learned to pump our toes into the snow on a steep ascent, heels on the descent...unless the slope was clear of rocks and boulders and then we bum-slid the whole length down (far faster than you can snake your way through powder). We roamed glaciers where we learned how to safely explore crevasses and millwells. And we learned how to sure-foot through shale by cutting an angle in a traverse in one direction, then another, until we'd scaled the whole peak

and stood on top of the world.

From there you see the familiar mountains stretching in every direction as far as forever. But you see so much more than you see in winter. Naked, without their white uniforms, the mountains reveal their secrets: turquoise glacial lakes banked by blazing fireweed and lichen-covered rocks; milky white alpine lakes; waterfalls that drop into dark silent pools. The views took my breath—and my heart—away.

But nothing was as challenging, or as moving, as the day I climbed Pigeon Spire, a finger pointing straight to heaven and requiring ropes, crampons and ice axes as well as more courage and resolve than I knew I had. It was all thanks to the guide, who believed in me more than I did and so inspired me to outdo myself, and to another Heli-Hiker/Skier out for his maiden voyage, too. In one 13-hour day he became a part of my life forever. In climbing, how much you commit/trust yourself to your partners determines how much you all get out of it.

I don't remember as much about the top of Pigeon Spire as what came before and after. Reaching the summit was just the bonus; it was the whole, long route that counted. Climbing is an athletic experience, to be sure, but it is a very personal and intellectual one, more so than even skiing the trees. You have to think with every inch of your body every inch of the way. It is at once exhilarating and draining, both physically and emotionally. And like Heli-Skiing in these mountains, it too, can become a necessary obsession.

(above)
Eric Unterberger, I.F.M.G.A., A.C.M.G. Mountain Guide

The Author
Catherine Ettlinger is a media consultant living in Los Angeles and New York City.

Pigeon Spire (2972m) in the Bugaboos

At CMH you get all the thrill of the climb without the agony of the approach march or descent. Now that's my kind of mountaineering!!! — Jon Howell

Jon Howell, Weston, Connecticut, was on the first mountaineering and hiking trip in the Cariboos.

(top) Guide, Pat Baird, belays two climbers to the summit of Centre Peak, Vowell Group. The Bugaboos are behind.

(bottom) Ernst Buehler, mountain guide, leads guests through the frozen "waves" of the Canoe Glacier in the Cariboos.

(opposite) Family rock climbing in the Adamants

A Perfect Day of Mountaineering

Diny Harrison, first fully-certified, North American female mountain guide, shows the ropes.

The mountaineering program was created to satisfy the needs of CMH's hiking guests who wanted more — more skills, more challenges, more accomplishments, more "mountains" to climb in every sense of the word. With the assistance of CMH's qualified guides, mountaineering changes from an intimidating concept to an exhilarating adventure — an adventure filled with emotions ranging from nervousness and apprehension to laughter and a profound sense of satisfaction.

Stretch the body and the mind will follow.

Kicking steps in early morning snow

Moving "short-roped" along a narrow ridge

Going higher to reach the peak

More vertical...more views

A secure and welcome belay

The final ridge before the summit

Reaching the top

Celebrating the challenge, the accomplishment...and the fun!

Family Adventure in the Adamants

The best part of CMH Heli-Hiking is exploring, hanging out with the guides, riding in the helicopter, the crafts and making new friends. — Krista Borgers

Krista, nine years old, is from Santa Barbara, California

The Conrad Glacier in the Bobbie Burns

*This makes going to work next Monday
awfully difficult.* — Betty Stephenson

Betty Stephenson, New Freedom, Pennsylvania,
celebrated her 20th wedding anniversary with her
husband Phil on a Heli-Hiking vacation.

A Guide Ruminates About a First-Time Mountaineer

by Ian Campbell

During your last ski week you picked up a Heli-Hiking brochure in the lodge, talked to one of the guides, and went ahead and booked a trip. Your only hesitation: after an awesome week of skiing, how could the summer trip compare?

After flying to the lodge, getting outfitted with boots, pack and all necessary gear, it's time to re-board the helicopter. Destination: a ridge-top in the high alpine. You asked to be in the fastest of the four groups, but one of the guys runs marathons and now you're not so sure.

It turns out that you're in better shape than you thought, and following the first brisk hike, as you wait at the top for the rest of the group, the guide asks if you would like to go climbing. Before you have time to think, the old skier-self from years ago blurts out "SURE!" You don't know it yet, but you may have just double-dared yourself into the best thing you'll ever do.

That evening, in the gear room, you're fitted with a harness, helmet, ice axe, and crampons. "They really do use this stuff," you think to yourself as one of the hikers peers into the room. "So, you're one of the climbers." Feeling unworthy of the recognition you mumble, "I guess so, I'm not sure yet."

The next day dawns early. Following breakfast, you and two other not-so-sure-wanabees climb aboard the helicopter for a flight to the foot of a glacier. Landing at

2440m, dazzled by the cool blue light of this amazing summer morning in the Selkirks, you watch as the helicopter descends the long valley. The lodge is still partly shrouded in the morning mist that rises slowly from the creek on cloudless mornings like this.

The guide comments that the clear night and cool temperatures have frozen the snow. Putting on crampons and tying to the rope for glacier travel, you begin the three-hour approach up the icy, blue-green tongue over snow-turned-to-ice that fell before Columbus was a sailor. This frozen world of high glacial neve, where you skirt crevasses and ice falls, has led to a narrow rock ridge. The arête rises in several steps toward the summit, nearly 300m above.

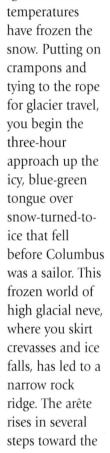

Following a brief break, you remove your crampons and the spacing between you and the others on the rope is shortened to make travel easier on the rock. Moving slowly, you alternate between going one at a time over the steeper parts and going as a group. You think to yourself, "My mother wouldn't like this."

The exposure is awesome, conjuring up mixed emotions: a strange sense of exhilaration and intimidation at the same time. You reach the summit. "Congratulations, you've almost made it." You look around for a higher point, relieved there's none. The guide adds, "You still have to get down...it ain't over 'til it's over." Pulling a

massacred sandwich from your pack, you reflect that it was only a few hours ago that you donned crampons for the first time. It might just be the best damned sandwich you ever ate, sitting on the summit with three others, eating in silence, still roped together staring out at this amazing place.

A short summit snooze, followed by some hero photos, and the descent begins. A rappel down the west face leads to a free hanging drop into a moat at the top of a steep snow slope. Twenty-four hours ago, this would have seemed crazy. Removing the rope, the guide turns with a smile..."Sayonara." Half standing, half tumbling he glissades down to where the angle lessens. Like a lemming you follow, jumping onto the steep snow. Warp eight, then yard sale. If you weren't so tired, you'd run up and do it again. Down, down to where snow thins to rock and rock to meadow, a lake beckons. Steaming boots and clothes stripped, you dive in head first. As your hands make contact with the icy blue liquid, a twinge of regret passes over you. Surfacing, and swimming to the shore, faster than you ever thought possible, you howl at the top of your lungs—for the cold...for the echo...just for the heck of it.

As the helicopter approaches to bring you back to the lodge, the guide, pointing out the route, comments,

"We've covered a lot of ground today." You agree, but in your soul, you know that you're not talking about the same thing. This adventure has given your life new meaning.

Back at the lodge, the hiker from the night before asks, "How was the climb?" "Not bad," you reply. "We're off to something even more challenging tomorrow."

(above)
Mountaineering guests are provided with crampons and ice axes for safe glacier travel.

(opposite) A mountain guide's tools of trade include a rack of slings, carabiners — and friends!

The Author
Ian Campbell, I.F.M.G.A. and A.C.M.G. Mountain Guide, is the manager of the Gothics Lodge.

(top) Keep your binoculars ready!

(bottom) "Little Creek" in the Adamants

(opposite) Premier Range in the Cariboo Mountains

(pg 50) Snow sliding!

(pg 51) "Kick Off" meadow below the Howser Spires in the Bugaboos

We crossed another glacier, navigated boulder fields, and then as if to accentuate the Zen nature of our accomplishment, traversed a valley forest dark and rich with the earthy scent of conifers and orchestrated by gently flowing streams reminiscent of a Japanese temple. — Bruce Allen

(top) "Anthea's" above Conrad Glacier in the Bobbie Burns

(bottom) Glacial seracs

(opposite) Monkey flowers

How CMH Mountaineering Changed My Life

by Steve Hiro

Driving from Banff to Calgary, with the spectacular snow-covered peaks in the rear-view mirror, I was struck by mixed emotions. Returning home from a vacation had never left me feeling this way before. Usually, I looked forward to getting back to the old routines, but not this time. It was then I knew that something special had happened Heli-Hiking in the Bugaboos.

It was one of a series of well-planned (my wife is a genius) and anxiously anticipated family vacations. Our itinerary included a western approach to the mountains from Edmonton, brief but invigorating stops at Jasper, Emerald Lake and Lake Louise, and an "unknown" experience, Heli-Hiking in the Bugaboos. After a stimulating flight from the staging area at Spillimacheen to the lodge, we settled in beneath the awesome spires of the Bugaboos with our most gracious hosts and fellow hikers.

During the first few days, we enjoyed jaunts through the varied terrain of this inspiring area: meadows and glaciers, ridges and cirques.

Then, one of the guides kindly recognized in me a need to do something more challenging and offered, for the final day, a chance to climb Pigeon Spire. I, along with another chosen hiker and our guide, awoke early the next morning and flew by helicopter, landing on Vowell Glacier, before the other guests were even awake. The day was clear and cool and promised to be unique.

After a two-hour walk on the glacier, roped up for safety, we arrived at the base of Pigeon Spire. I had no previous experience in technical mountaineering or rock climbing, but did bring loads of enthusiasm and reasonable physical condition to the task. The day turned out to be all that it promised and we spent a good part of it summiting the spire as we were overcoming our fears of height and exposure. What an incredible feeling sitting on the top of a peak, looking out, smug but wildly content with accomplishment!

The descent and walk out were equally challenging and fulfilling and we returned to the lodge late in the evening, tattered and tired but forever changed.

Returning to Florida with this melancholy, I began to recognize a new-found attachment to the mountains and hoped, perhaps, to find a way in the future to become more a part of them. I am happy to report that I developed the inspiration and the courage to move to northwestern Montana, an area quite similar in terrain to the Canadian Rockies. My interest in climbing has blossomed (now at level 5.9) and I am enjoying most other aspects of mountain life.

I often now have snow-covered peaks in my rear-view mirror, but the melancholy has been replaced with a profound satisfaction. For, you see, there are also mountains through the front and side windows as well.

(above)
Celebrating the day's accomplishments

The Author
Steve Hiro is a cardiovascular surgeon who now lives in Missoula, Montana.

Roko Koell, mountain guide, leading a climb in the Bugaboos

We disembarked on the narrow runway of Pyrite Ridge...Here we pick our way over ground littered with acres of splintered shale. It's as if the gods had thrown a wild party and smashed all their dinner plates. The shale tinkles like wind chimes in a breeze after each of our footsteps. — Tom Dunkel

Tom Dunkel writing about Heli-Hiking in *National Geographic Traveler*.

(top) Scoping the views in the Cariboos

(bottom) Margaret and Hans Gmoser during the 20th Anniversary celebration in the Cariboo Mountains

(opposite) Crossing a glacial stream in an alpine meadow in the Adamants

Your ability and willingness to accommodate a wide range of ages and wants was impressive. Don't change a thing. — Ken Brody

Ken Brody lives in Raleigh, North Carolina

(top) Time for a refreshing dip!

(bottom) Fleabane

We came. We saw. We hiked. And all we want to do is come back!

An anonymous notation in the Guest Book at the Bobbie Burns Lodge.

(top) View from Silver Shadow in the Adamants

(bottom) Lady slipper

A Heli-Hiking Field Trip

One of the true pleasures of experiencing the alpine wilderness is when you become actively engaged with the new, exciting world around you. With the assistance of the experienced CMH mountain guides, this new world is brought into close focus. Floral details are explained; geological oddities are pointed out; ecological systems are discussed — and all of this at the time you are holding a piece of this reality in your own hands.

The field trip illustrated here is but one example of the kind of experience that awaits the CMH Heli-Hiker.

Approaching one of the innumerable, unnamed waterfalls in a valley basin in the Adamants

The guide provides a general overview on the geology of the basin

Walking into the upper reaches of the basin

The second shower of the day!

A close examination of the power of water as an agent of erosion

A hands-on lesson...

...on the composition of...

...alpine soil.

A classic example of the metamorphic composition of the Columbia Range

Capturing millions of years of geologic change

Off to another adventure!

(top) Willy Trinker, mountain guide, and his group cele-brate the day.

(bottom) "The pilot pulls back on the throttle, and the helicopter touches down with all the fury of an autumn leaf falling from a tree." — Tom Dunkel

(pg 64) Glacial action has starkly revealed the "zebra" stripes of a sedimentary rock in the Bobbie Burns.

(pg 65) Early summer run-off through Septet Basin in the Bugaboos

(top) Heli-Napping!

(bottom) Alpine Helicopter's pilot, Dave Mulock

Our guide informed us that we were among a group of only 200 people who in the past 20 years were able to be in Joy Valley during the summer due to the extreme mosquito problem. But the night before gave off a frost and a light snow that got rid of the pests. It was a very special time to spend with my dad walking and exploring the lakes, streams, marshes, and waterfalls coming off the glaciers. — Richard Shrader

Richard Shrader, Torrance, California, has skied with CMH for over 20 years. Richard brought his 85-year-old father Heli-Hiking to share his passion for the mountain experience.

Two hundred years amounts to temporal chump change here. This is a still-primordial landscape gouged out of the Earth's crust ages ago by glacial action, of mountains thrust up into being by the slow-motion collision of subterranean tectonic plates, of delicate mosses and lichens that can take several decades to grow an inch. — Tom Dunkel

(top) Cobalt Lake in the Bugaboos

(bottom) Happy Heli-Hikers!

(opposite) One of Valemount's many scenic views

Buck Corrigan, mountain guide, assists with lunch at CMH's Family Adventure in the Adamants.

We hiked the same mountains Bill skis. The scenery, the food, the lodging, the fun, the new friends we made — our adventure was magnificent. Enough so that we booked again for the following summer's vacation. Heli-Hiking provided me with an incredible opportunity to understand why Bill is so passionate and obsessed about his Heli-Ski trips. — Kathy Borgers

Kathy Borgers lives with her husband and two children in Santa Barbara, California.

The young and the brave

It was everything Bill described. My sensors were on overload. I felt so alive. I pushed myself physically beyond what I thought I was capable of. I experienced the great Canadian Mountain Holiday.

— Kathy Borgers

71

As we fly across the valley, I note how long we're actually in the air: about two minutes, 50 seconds. It would take a fit man at least a full-day of hard hiking to cover the same distance on foot. — Tom Dunkel

(top) Safety first! Alpine Helicopter's mountain-trained pilots fly more than 4,500 guests each summer.

(bottom) Kimmel Glacier, the Cariboos

I had always wanted my wife MaryAnne to see the beautiful mountains and valleys we ski in the winter. — John Howell

(top) Exploring the mountains includes time to relax

(bottom) Moss campion

(pg 74) Septet Basin in the Septet Range of the Bugaboos

73

Guests Sarah and Philip Hine take a short break.

We sprawl on the grass and tuck into our lunch bags. Excercise and mountain air have made us ravenous and we joke that we'll all go home with "Heli-bellies." — Anita Draycott

Anita Draycott is the Editorial Director, Special Editions, of Chatelaine magazine.

Twenty years of CMH Heli-Hiking

(top) In 1998, Cariboo Lodge hosted a five-day celebration of the 20th Anniversary of CMH Heli-Hiking with Tauck Tours. Left to right: Ethan Compton, Geoff Powter, Christie McLaren, Lloyd Gallagher, Sharon Firth, Hans Gmoser, Linda Heywood, Margaret Gmoser.

(bottom) Nicole Laliberte, one of the first employees at the Cariboo Lodge, has been the house manager since 1977.

(opposite) Hans Gmoser guides his group above the Canoe Glacier in the Cariboos.

(opposite inset) Ethan Compton, Hans Gmoser's original benefactor in the creation of Canadian Mountain Holidays

(pp 78/79) Seen here from CMH Valemount area, Mt. Robson (3954m) is the highest peak in the Canadian Rockies.

"Walking along the ridge gave me the feeling that at any moment Julie Andrews would be nearby singing 'The Hills are Alive With the Sound of Music.' No matter where you looked you couldn't take your eyes off Mt. Robson standing 50 miles to the east."

Richard Shrader

The flight home to the luxury of the lodge

Photo Credits

Aerial Innovations
John Bilodeau
Gary Brettnacher
Dave Butler
Halle Flygare
Torsten Geldsetzer
Kevin Hasson
Roko Koell
Kim Laker
Roger Laurilla
Patrick Morrow
Alec Pytlowany
Scott Rowed
Brad White
Elizabeth Wiltzen